ECCLES

THE BEGINNING OF THE ECCLESIA

JOHN METCALFE

Printed and Published by
John Metcalfe Publishing Trust
Church Road, Tylers Green
Penn, Buckinghamshire

—

© John Metcalfe Publishing Trust 1990
All Rights Reserved

—

First Published August 1990

—

ISBN 1 870039 25 4

—

Price 10p

—

The content of this tract appears as the sixth chapter in the book 'The Church: What is it?' and ought to be considered in that context. For a full exposition of the doctrine, see 'The Church: What is it?', The Publishing Trust.

THE BEGINNING OF THE ECCLESIA

IT cannot be over-emphasized that the *ecclesia* of Christ, the assembly, is entirely new: nothing remotely like it existed prior to the day of Pentecost and the giving of the Holy Ghost. Christ's assembly is not in any sense a continuation of old testament Israel and its assembly.

In the one case Jehovah was veiled, and in thick darkness. In the other, the God and Father of our Lord Jesus Christ has been revealed in radiant light. One was earthly, the other heavenly. One was carnal, the other spiritual.

The one was temporal, the other is eternal. One was under the law, the other delivers from the law. In the one case the people were kept at forbidding distance by a mediatorial priesthood. In the other case the people have been brought within the sanctuary, and have become the priesthood.

One people was condemned by Moses through the legal commandment; the other has been justified by grace through the faith of Jesus Christ.

In the one testament God's wrath was kindled, the people were cursed, and the law was a ministration of death. In the other testament God has been appeased, the people are blessed, and the gospel is nothing but a savour of life unto life to all the heirs of promise. Just no compatibility between the two, no compatibility at all.

On every count the new testament *ecclesia* is a wholly new thing.

Yet the truth is, in most principles, and many respects, present-day Christendom appears closer to the legal system of earthly Israel, with its bondage to the priestly ministrations of man, than it does to the glorious grace of the heavenly *ecclesia*, with its liberty under the divine ministry of the Son of God.

Then, a new work is needed, and should be expected, recovering to our own day all that has been lost since the beginning.

When the Father revealed the Son to Peter at Caesarea Philippi, this brought to light a mystery which had been hidden from ages and generations, from the very foundation of the world.

This prophetic vision of the Son—although given before the cross—actually presumed his having been crucified, raised from the dead, ascended and seated as Son in the glory, in manhood, on behalf of his people. It presumed the Holy Ghost having been poured out from heaven to fill the *ecclesia* on earth.

That is the nature, as it is the character, of Christ's assembly: it is an entirely new, divine, heavenly, spiritual, supernatural, and glorious mystery.

Christ's assembly did not exist before, save in the eternal purpose of God, Father, Son, and Holy Ghost. But the atonement having been made, propitiation effected, redemption accomplished, justification wrought, righteousness imputed, the Spirit outpoured, the Father and his children —the *huiothesia*—were made one in divine and heavenly glory in Christ.

Christ being risen from the dead, the people for whom he died, seen as having died in him, necessarily were viewed in the counsels of God as raised up together with Christ from the grave.

The Son being ascended to his Father and their Father, his God and their God, he and his people being all of one, it followed also that they were viewed in God's purpose as ascended and seated together with him.

Before the *ecclesia* even began, therefore, this was its position, achieved vicariously by the death, burial, resurrection, and ascension of the Son of God. Hence, Christ ascended, the Spirit given, there came to pass the beginning of the fulfilment of the saying of Jesus at Caesarea Philippi, 'Upon this rock I will build my assembly.'

'Upon this rock'—that is, the rock of the revelation of the Son by his Father in heaven, drawing to the Son those whom he had chosen according to his own divine purpose and election in Christ.

'I will build'—not, 'I have built', or 'I continue building': which might have seemed to have applied to Israel, or to appear to have some continuity with what went before; but, 'I will build'. This refers to a future, new, different, work, about to begin in the manner made conspicuous by the Father's heavenly revelation to Peter.

'I will build my *ecclesia*'—then, this was the beginning of the *ecclesia*. This therefore must be the point, and the only conceivable point throughout time to the very end, I say, this must be the point of reference to which all must be brought, and by which all must be tried thereafter.

It was not that Jehovah had not wrought in Israel, or, indeed, throughout the old testament: he had. But he had not wrought this.

Now, through the Father's revelation from heaven of the Son by the Holy Ghost, a new work was to commence. An entirely new creation from God out of heaven would have its beginning.

This work would originate individually with the Father's revelation of the Son from heaven. The Son, recognising and receiving every one in whom this work had been wrought, would by the Holy Ghost from heaven build in, and build up, all those taught of the Father to come to him. The result of this building work he called, and calls, 'My *ecclesia*'.

The watershed was the day of Pentecost. That was the true beginning.

To that beginning everything that is subsequent ought to be true, for to it all must be brought, and by it every single word and work shall be judged at the last day.

It is therefore vital to understand the beginning of the *ecclesia*, and the *ecclesia* in the beginning. Everything since is totally irrelevant. Irrelevant? Yes, because everything since must itself be judged by the same one—and only—criterion.

Then what of the work of God before the existence of the *ecclesia*, in the days of the old testament?

Before, from the times of the patriarchs, God had wrought salvation in the earth. Before, God indeed had his people, just as much called his saints as those of the new testament.

He was their Saviour. By him they had been alarmed, awakened, convicted, and quickened. From him was their faith, their repentance, their righteousness, their obedience, their love, their hope, and their endurance. Of this the Spirit bears testimony in the eleventh chapter of the epistle to the Hebrews.

They were a regenerate people, Jehovah had quickened them to life. He was their light and their salvation. From him they received their help, for he was the Mighty One of Jacob. He was the saving strength of Israel.

All this is clear, never more so than in the psalms. But all this was either an individual work wrought in the patriarchs, or that wrought in the saints of Jehovah on earth in Israel within the confines of the old covenant and under the constrictions of the old law.

Now the veil of the temple has been rent in twain from the top to the bottom, the earth has been shaken, and the rocks have been rent. Now the darkness is past and the true light shines. Now even the dead have been raised to life again. If so, the *new* testament has begun.

God has gone up with a shout, the LORD with the sound of a trumpet. Heaven rings with the shouting of victory. God has triumphed gloriously, God sitteth upon the throne of his holiness.

Now Christ has ascended on high, all righteousness fulfilled. God's righteousness is declared for the remission of sins that are past. The Father has been glorified in the Son, and the Son has been glorified by the Father.

Christ is seated on the throne of his Father. The new work is wrought from heaven by the Son, glorified in manhood, a divine work, a heavenly work, an everlasting work: the work of Christ in building his own *ecclesia*.

The *new* testament has commenced, and it has proved new beyond all that eye could see, or ear could hear, beyond all that ever did, or ever could, enter into the heart of man to conceive. This is the beginning of the *ecclesia*.

The beginning of the *ecclesia* commenced with the baptism of the Holy Ghost.

This had been foretold by John the Baptist: 'He that sent me to baptize with water, the same said unto me, Upon whom thou shalt see the Spirit descending, and remaining on him, the same is he which baptizeth with the Holy Ghost. And I saw, and bare record that this is the Son of God.'

This baptism, which brings in Christ's *ecclesia*, and which brings into Christ's *ecclesia*, this baptism, I say, took place on the day of Pentecost. This was the day on which the Son of God poured out the Holy Ghost from heaven, who, descending, filled the whole company.

The baptism of the Spirit therefore is corporate.

The baptism of the Spirit is for the company, or to bring one individually into that company.

'For by one Spirit are we all baptized into one body, whether we be Jews or Gentiles, whether we be bond or free; and have been all made to drink into one Spirit.'

By this baptism the Holy Ghost himself fills the *ecclesia*. By the fulness of the Holy Ghost in the *ecclesia*, Christ indwells his own assembly. By the indwelling of the Son within that assembly, the habitation of God and the Father is made complete.

Here is the fulfilling of the house of God, which is the *ecclesia* of the living God, the pillar and ground of the truth.

It is the oneness of God in Father, Son, and Holy Ghost that is manifest in the *ecclesia*. God dwells in his assembly, and only his assembly, the world being void of his presence.

By this divine indwelling—from which the whole world is excluded—the entire *ecclesia* has the testimony of being the only habitation of God. But the whole world has nothing at all that is of God.

The world is therefore convinced by the power and witness of the Spirit come down from heaven to dwell in Christ's *ecclesia*. Convinced, that is, by so palpable a divine presence in the assembly. Whereas the world, void of that divine presence, has nothing but emptiness in itself.

'If I go not away, the Comforter will not come unto you: but if I depart, I will send him unto you. And when he is come, he will'—by no more than the fulness of his presence in the entire *ecclesia*, over against his total absence from the whole world—'he will reprove the world of sin, and of righteousness, and of judgment.'

'Of sin, because they believe not on me'. But the *ecclesia* believes on him, and the Spirit's powerful presence fills and indwells the *ecclesia*, clearly endorsing that belief. But he does not endorse the unbelieving world, which is altogether void of his presence.

But why not? Because they do not believe on the Christ, the Son of the living God.

'Of righteousness, because I go to my Father'. He goes, that is, having first brought in justifying righteousness by the shedding of his blood on behalf of all who believe, but of none who disbelieve. Thus it is that Christ goes to the

Father, who sends the Spirit to the justified assembly, but denies him to the condemned world.

The Spirit fills the one, and leaves the other empty. This convinces the world of righteousness having been wrought on behalf of the Spirit-filled assembly, but not for the self-justifying world.

'Of judgment, because the prince of this world is judged'. The world denied the true Christ. The world hopes for another Christ—more compatible with its taste—yet to come. Thus the world denied not only the Son but the Father which sent him. The world owns—but in different forms, by various paths, in diverse ways—one god. But it was in the name of their one god, and for his service, that the world crucified the Son.

But the baptism of the Spirit was upon the *ecclesia*. Not upon the world. Then who was the god of this world?

Their god was the prince of this world, who had just been judged. That convinced them of judgment.

It was not so much what was preached. It was not so much the apostles' doctrine. It was the fulness of the presence of the Holy Ghost in the whole assembly, and his total absence from the whole world. That in itself convinced the world not only of sin, not only of righteousness, but of coming judgment on all the earth and on the spirit that was in it, besides every worldly system, religious, political, and social.

This sharp almost tangible difference between the assembly and the world will and must appear whenever and wherever Christ builds his assembly.

Otherwise, of what worth are his words?

But his words are invaluable, and hence, always come to pass. If they do not come to pass in the denominations, sects, organisations and assemblies of men, for all their presumptuous claims, theories and doctrines, there can be but one conclusion: *they* are the builders, and the builders of a dead, unendorsed religion.

As for him, *he* is the Stone which these builders rejected. And that rejection is the norm of this present day, in terms of the 'church'. Save for a few, very few, separated and gathered saints.

However, the more the truth is fearlessly held forth, the more the Spirit will baptize into one body, and the more we shall see by faith with our own eyes the result of the fact that Christ repeats this day these words from heaven 'Upon this rock I will build my *ecclesia*'.

From everlasting to everlasting the *ecclesia* abides a heavenly and divine concept, to which in time the assembly on earth, filled with the the Holy Ghost, conforms.

It was but one. It must be one. The *ecclesia* answered in unity as a body to the Head, as a bride to the Husband, as a household to the Father, as a city to the King, as a temple to the Holy Ghost. One assembly.

This was most clearly seen in the very beginning at Jerusalem. There was but one pool of light, it was the one *ecclesia*. Elsewhere all the world, every nation, all religion, to the ends of the earth, lay in thick darkness.

The whole world lay in wickedness, under the power of darkness, beneath the sentence of death. But out of the *ecclesia*, the perfection of beauty, God shined. This one place on earth, the assembly at Jerusalem, was full of light, life, and love, it was filled with heavenly glory radiating the divine presence of God, Father, Son, and Holy Ghost.

There was nothing else anywhere on earth. Nothing but darkness, blackness, deadness, and condemnation, throughout all nations, in all the world. All that there was, that was of God, existed in that one company at Jerusalem.

That was the *ecclesia*. If any were to be saved, they must be added to that. 'And the Lord added to the *ecclesia* daily such as should be saved.' As to every other creature under heaven, 'Of the rest durst no man join himself to them.'

Then came an apparent change, but it was not a real change. As the *ecclesia* increased by the going forth of the word of God, saints were gathered in other localities, too far from Jerusalem to meet with the assembly. A new thing occurred: *ecclesiai*. 'The assemblies'.

But this altered nothing in heaven. It made absolutely no difference to the heavenly concept. No difference to the Father. No difference to the Son. No difference to the Holy Ghost. No difference to Christ's *ecclesia*.

It was simply that the unity of that entity, that one heavenly concept, was now reflected in a manifold way: but it was still *that* which was reflected. It was, it is, and it ever shall be, but one *ecclesia*. The fact that the light of that one *ecclesia* shone forth in several assemblies altered nothing. The light remained just as one as the divine Person from whom it shone. No matter how many assemblies, there remained but one divine radiance.

The *concept* of the assembly appears always as one, no matter how many the assemblies. It continues that 'Upon this rock I will build my *ecclesia*', singular. The 'assemblies' do not alter that: they magnify it.

In fact the plural 'churches' does not occur until Acts 9:31. Thirty-six times the word is in the plural. Twice there is reference to 'every' assembly. Often 'the' *ecclesia* is used in the sense of one of the assemblies, as, 'the' *ecclesia* of the Thessalonians, 'the' assembly which is in Smyrna. Here the reference is to that particular one of the assemblies. But this does not alter the essential nature of the assembly of Christ as one assembly.

It *is* one assembly, irrespective of the multiplying of the testimony.

It is nothing other than the one assembly that is manifested by an assembly in such and such a place. It is *that* assembly in such and such a place.

Christ's *ecclesia* is ever one; indivisible. Wherever he should build his *ecclesia*, the *whole entity* is made manifest by his building in *that* place. It is *the* assembly that is seen there. 'The assembly of God which is at Corinth.' One God; one assembly. The assembly of God.

By the continuous disintegration of Protestantism into denominationalism, sectarianism, and independency—coupled with growing worldliness, indifference, and apathy—more than anything, the concept of the one assembly has been quite lost.

But when the apostle declared Christ to be 'Head over all things to *the* assembly', Eph. 1:22, here was no future ideal for the coming inheritance in glory. The apostle meant *now*.

What horror, then, would have taken hold upon Paul had he known that this precious doctrine was to be perverted into an empty theory for each division to rationalize as its own justification. A meaningless thought about which disobedient evangelicalism would utter its platitudes as it drifted even further into apostasy. The truth reveals that the *ecclesia* is a reality from which Protestantism, in its latter-day disobedience, has utterly departed.

In the beginning of the *ecclesia* the truth of Christ's Headship was actually realised in all the assemblies. Each assembly showed forth that one assembly over which Christ was Head.

Not merely to one of the assemblies, but to *the* assembly the following words of Paul are directed: 'To the intent that now'—not in eternity; not *only* at the beginning; *now* —'unto the principalities and powers in heavenly places might be known by the assembly the manifold wisdom of God', Eph. 3:10.

Now, although there were many assemblies, the assembly was but one, and the many assemblies were to show forth that oneness, and all heaven was to see it. Principalities and powers in heavenly places were to see it. To this end the assemblies on earth were to view themselves in a heavenly, not an earthly light. They were to see themselves as observed from heaven. For in the beginning they were not disobedient to the heavenly vision.

But this is a disobedient and gainsaying people, an evil generation, becoming the worse as the 'churches'—by which they mean their divided denominations—justify their unbelief and hardness of heart with a profession of Christ, and a veneer of scriptural quotations. Nevertheless all power is given to the Son, in heaven and on earth. And this, to the end of the age. The very end. So that in spite of all the working of man, we may boldly trust in that unchangeable word which shall stand even until the last day: 'I *will* build my assembly'!

And what could be more certain than the steadfast faithfulness of the Son of God, even to the very end, seeing that this fidelity springs from his everlasting love for his own *ecclesia*: 'Christ loved the assembly, and gave himself for it.'

This *ecclesia* or assembly of Christ is not some intangible fantasy of the disobedient 'evangelicals'—such as J.C. Ryle, an Anglican 'bishop' appointed by Disraeli, who believed nothing, to spite Gladstone, who was a high churchman—inventing an 'invisible church' with visible members permanently scattered among all denominations!

But still Christ builds his own *ecclesia*, which, though built spiritually, is built on earth. This is *the* assembly. Unscriptural philosophizing about 'the church militant', or 'the church triumphant', is wholly to be rejected. *The* assembly is the light which all the assemblies show forth, and with which each one is radiant. This light of the glory, shining in the face of Jesus Christ, is that of one Head, one body, one *ecclesia*, dwelling in one Spirit, and indwelt by one God and Father.

This light—not talk about it—is what needs to be recovered in our day, and it is what should be looked for, and inwardly expected, by the faithful remnant. When these things are so, then the modern priests, scribes, Pharisees, lawyers, Herodians, Sadducees, doctors, rabbis—not to mention know-all Brethren, with their hard hearts, cold affections, and heads full of dead and self-righteous theories—will surely rage. Let them rage! Let them storm, slander, lie, persecute, do what they will. What care we for that? Nothing at all.

In the beginning each assembly answered to *the* assembly. And *the* assembly answered to each assembly. This is a heavenly vision: 'A glorious *ecclesia*'. Eph. 5:27.

This glorious assembly abides as one in heaven with the Lord, whilst one on earth in the midst of tears and tribulation. This oneness is shown forth in every single assembly, the oneness of heavenly union between Christ and his bride, the Head and the body. 'I speak concerning Christ and the assembly.' Each and every one of the assemblies shows forth *nothing less* than this whole, though it be by but two or three gathered in his name.

'He is the Head of the body, the *ecclesia*', Col. 1:18. I fulfil this ministry, said the apostle, 'for his body's sake, which is the *ecclesia*', Col. 1:24. Just as it was written of Jesus 'The zeal of thine house hath eaten me up'. So this same holy zeal consumed Paul.

How clear the apostle's vision! nothing less than all saints, every member of the body of Christ, the entire heavenly *ecclesia*. How fervent his love: in stripes, in imprisonments, in persecutions, in perils oft; yet his ardour remained unabated. How consuming was his ministry: day and night with tears, labouring in word and doctrine, Paul was indefatigable in this ministry 'for his body's sake'.

Never once was Paul's vision dimmed. Never once was his love quenched. Never once did he limit or constrain his ministry to a party. His ministry was 'for his body's sake, which is the *ecclesia*.'

The assembly, which is his body, is heavenly, it is one, it is in divine union, and *it* is seen and shown forth in all the assemblies gathered by Christ into the one assembly, the one fellowship of the mystery, and in none other.

This is the *ecclesia* as it was in the beginning. There is none other, there never will be any other, and there never will be the remotest shadow of turning from what was in the beginning, even to the very end, on the part of the heavenly Builder.

All the shadows, and all the turning, are on the part of the professions and confessions of Christ that fall short of the truth, or in the parties and divisions that miss the mark of the *ecclesia* built by Christ alone. All these have come in since the beginning. But there was no need for it. And there is even less need for it to continue now.

Whilst the history of the beginning of the *ecclesia* appears in the Acts of the Apostles, the doctrine is unfolded in the succeeding epistles.

It was by the apostolic ministry that Christ raised up the *ecclesia*.

Hence the book of Acts is called 'The Acts of the Apostles'. The book is not called 'The Acts of the Holy Ghost'. Nor even 'The Acts of Christ'. Though every divine work recorded in the Acts came from Christ on high by the Spirit below. But it came from him through the apostolic ministry below. He acted through the ministry of the apostles. Thus the record is called 'The Acts of the Apostles'.

It is true that the saints 'went everywhere preaching the word'. But it is equally true that this was neither their choice nor their doing, it was the result of the persecution. They did not initiate it, it happened to them. They fled the persecution. That was how they came to travel abroad. In consequence they testified. That is, they went everywhere preaching the *apostolic* word which they had been taught, and in which they had been nourished and brought up under the ministry.

Having gone forth as a result of the persecution, scattered by the providence of God, so the word sprang up among the Gentiles. In consequence the great apostle of the

Gentiles was raised up and sent forth from Christ in heaven, with a unique ministry, to edify and build up the *ecclesia* among all nations.

This is hardly 'The Acts of the Brethren'. Such acts, springing as they do from the will of man which cannot stand being subordinate to the ministry, will never build up Christ's *ecclesia*. They will pull it down. Brethrenism is in the very teeth of scripture at the salient point of the ministry. The record refutes them: It is the Acts of the *Apostles*; it is not The Acts of the *Brethren*. Why not? Because Christ does not use brethren as such to build up his *ecclesia*, he uses the apostolic ministry. Then brethren are built up, and so God has ordained it, for thus the body is brought to the 'edification of itself in love'.

And, sending his ministers from heaven, as subject to the apostolic word, example, and doctrine, God continues the same acts in principle even until now. He never does, and he never will, vary from his own divine principles and terms. With him there is no variableness neither shadow of turning. Hence the saying, As it was in the beginning, is now, and ever shall be. Amen.

It goes without saying that the immutable divine principles and acts seen in the new testament scriptures are utterly different from all the humanly devised methods of subsequent ages. Never is this more true than of the ministry. The ministry of the new testament is clean contrary in principle to the hiring of some manufactured professional 'pastor' by a denominational, un-denominational, or inter-denominational organisation or congregation, which then has the impertinence to call him 'the minister' and themselves 'the church'.

No such thing existed in all the record of the new testament. None of the epistles addressed any such organisation, none addressed any such office, and none acknowledged any such system. Look and see.

In the beginning of the *ecclesia* God did something, not man. It was from heaven, not the earth. It was all of God's initiative, man had nothing to do with it. God wrought the work. The assembly and the assemblies were the result.

Unless today we come out of the division and confusion, the pretence and play acting, to be gathered as they were, under that ministry sent from heaven; or unless we will submit with meek penitence to being found in the way of it, calling upon God to work what we cannot; then we are at best little better than the foolish virgins with no oil in their vessels with their lamps, slumbering on in indifference. Then, like them, we shall surely awake at last to the dreadful reality, the reality which we refused to face as we trifled on in our journeying to that great and notable day of the Lord.

All that man builds, or can build, in a way of religion; all that he does, or can do, that conforms with scripture;

all his reforming, reviving, renewing, is nothing to the point. *Christ built his own ecclesia.* From heaven. And he still does. Not man. '*I will build* my assembly.'

Man builds nothing but earthly vanity and human pretence, scorning to become as humble as a little child, obstinately refusing to submit to Christ's building. Why? Because *man* wants to be the builder. Such men are afraid —not without good cause—that if they submit to him, they will be nothing more than the least of all, which is what their vanity and self-esteem cannot stand.

Hired 'ministers' may speak from the scriptures to the congregations which form their sects, but the scriptures were not given by the Holy Ghost to them, their congregations, or their sects, that they should so speak. Nor did the Lord from heaven put one such word, by the Spirit, into their mouths.

If they deny this, then let them tell us why they went to bible school, to learn how to substitute what man can manufacture, for what, in the beginning, the Lord himself did from heaven without human aid? Tell us? But we know. The Lord has not done it with *them*, and that is what they cannot stand. For they will be first, and they will have the chief seats in the synagogue. Hence they must force themselves to turn to man's substitutionary system, to do for them what the Lord did not do, and would not do. This is Saul's offspring.

Neither were the epistles written to them, their sects, their denominations, or their divisions, each single one of which separately calls itself 'the church'! As if these many misnamed divisions were in the same position or on the same basis as was the one *ecclesia* in the beginning! They were not, and they are not. They must all come down, like Zacchaeus, if the Lord is to do the work. For he shall do all of the work, or none of the work. But climbing down is the very thing that they have never done, and that they never will do.

Incumbent hirelings may speak to their paying audiences out of texts from Romans to Revelation. As though there were any relation between *their* 'ministry', and the ministry of those Spirit-filled, God-taught, divinely called ministers whom Christ sends from heaven! Or as if there were any comparison between *their* 'building', and the *ecclesia* built by Christ in the beginning!

The scriptures pertain neither to them, nor to their congregations. Neither does Christ put his word from heaven into the mouth of the one, nor write it upon the heart of the other, at any time. They should cease from fantasy, and admit reality. But they have not the humility.

The *ecclesia* in Acts was formed by the Holy Ghost from heaven, and the apostles in Acts were sent from the Lord in glory. And all this without the hand or work of man once appearing. Indeed, should the flesh have shown itself, immediately it would have been discerned, judged, and rejected. All was of God, first and last. And it still is. Nothing has happened that makes the least difference to anything that really matters.

The *ecclesia* in the beginning was supernatural: it was past the power of man to mimic. Men could not copy it, nor could they 'pattern' their religious organisations upon it. It was the assembly of God, for the very reason that God formed it for himself by himself as his own peculiar dwelling.

The fear of God rested upon this assembly. The power of God filled it. And there was a great fear of grieving, or in any way marring, the mighty power, influence, glory, and presence of the Holy Ghost from heaven, whose indwelling life was more tangible to them, and much more important, than their own existence.

Once given the descent of the Holy Ghost, and his Person filling the assembly, the power of union was present, uniting the saints in one body. The saints were then to be taught by the living ministry all the words of this life.

In consequence the saints hung on the apostles' doctrine in order to be nourished up in the life of the one body. All outside was barren: they needed to be fed within. All around was dark: they needed light in the way. All about was danger: they needed the trumpet blast of warning.

Baptized by one Spirit into one body, the saints sought earnestly for spiritual communion in the apostles' doctrine and fellowship, according to the anointing of the Holy One, concerning the common life of the members of that one body. Moreover, having been brought into the habitation of God through the Spirit, they must needs learn how to behave themselves in the house of God, which is the assembly of the living God, the pillar and ground of the truth.

The saints had been begotten by the incorruptible seed of the word of God. Then, as newborn babes, they craved with the earnest desire of life itself for that nourishment and admonition, chastisement and scourging, tribulation and patience, experience and hope, which would bring their newborn life to fulfilment; to attain to the maturity of sonship; to develop priestly discernment; and to have their senses exercised to discern both good and evil. Nothing but the heaven-sent apostolic ministry could provide for these deep-seated desires.

The record of this provision from on high may be found in the epistles. But these epistles were certainly not written to divided sects and denominations, with dead and worldly congregations, presided over by some salaried hireling. They were written by holy men of God to the *ecclesia* of the living God, gathered by the power and unity of the Spirit into one body.

The very idea that these epistles should have been appropriated by papists, Anglicans, and other denominational missions and sects—each to 'support' his own system!—as if any of them bore the least resemblance to the original recipients, would have filled the writers with horror.

And to this very day, such writings apply only to those gatherings which have the same character and distinctiveness as the one *ecclesia* to which they were addressed in the beginning.

The apostolic epistles were addressed to Christ's *ecclesia*, and to Christ's *ecclesia* alone, wherever that one body was represented locally. Such local assemblies never lost sight of *the* assembly, of which each was the one divine manifestation in that given locality. Neither did the saints ever lose sight of the ministry sent down from the one heavenly Head on high in the glory, to minister to the whole assembly filled by the one Person of the Spirit on earth below.

For the variously divided but uneasily confederate—though suspiciously jealous—'ministers' and 'pastors' of the denominations, sects and independencies, to use these epistles for their hire, why, this is to steal God's words indeed. It is to make trade of God's words—though they belong neither to them nor their employers—and it shall surely be required at the hand of every one of them in the last day.

For these are of the sort in whose mouth the Spirit did not put a single word at any one time. And their sects are those which the Spirit never gathered in any single instance.

Therefore, to speak of any of the epistles, from Romans to Revelation, as having the least bearing upon or relevance to the denominated and partial, not to mention worldly and carnal, sectarian gatherings—in divisions which they misname 'churches'—is nothing short of ridiculous.

Each epistle was written to Christ's *ecclesia*, with words which the Holy Ghost gave, framed from the lips of the Lord in glory, attested by the everlasting God, and set down by the pen of holy, faithful, and sent ministers. Unless men are in the light, life and power, that these ministers were, what have such words to do either with them, or with the divisions which hire them?

Heart-broken and penitent, with weeping and mourning, the saints are to be gathered out of all the sects and divisions, and from under all the dead hirelings. For these deny the unity of the body of Christ, shaming the Head of the *ecclesia*, stealing his names and words to describe themselves, when such names and words have nothing to do either with them or with their systems.

These things being so—and so late in the age—now, therefore, it is time to remember that the blessing rests upon such as the poor in spirit; upon those that mourn; upon the meek; upon all who hunger and thirst after righteousness. Such as these.

It is time to recall that of the many 'woes' pronounced by Christ, the 'woe' that he fastened upon the religious was against the 'rich', for they should be sent empty away; against the 'full', for want shall come upon them as an armed man; against the 'laughing', for there shall be weeping and gnashing of teeth; against those 'of whom all men speak well', for they shall hear the words, Depart from me, ye cursed.

Then it is time to heed the midnight cry, Behold, the bridegroom cometh! For the night is far spent. 'Behold, the bridegroom cometh, go ye out to meet him.' It is time to awake out of sleep. It is time to put on sackcloth and ashes. It is time to be poor; to hunger; to weep; to be hated of men; to be separated from their company; to be reproached of men; to have one's name cast out as evil, for the Son of man's sake. It is high time.

High time to repent. To become as little children. To mourn every one by himself apart. Surely this becomes us in these last days. For there are still conditions upon which the blessing is pronounced. These abide. They are the conditions to which the power of the Spirit is assured. 'For he saith, I have heard thee in a time accepted, and in the day of salvation have I succoured thee: behold, now is the accepted time; now is the day of salvation.'

With those in just such conditions, that is, from the Lord's poor, Christ builds his *ecclesia*. Why from those? Because in them already there is made manifest that prior work of God, which shall surely be followed by the revelation of his Son from heaven.

'Hear the word of the LORD, ye that tremble at his word; Your brethren that hated you, that cast you out for my name's sake, said, Let the LORD be glorified: but he shall appear to your joy, and they shall be ashamed.' Now, of those whom these hypocrites cast out, Christ shall build his *ecclesia*.

When Jesus had given sight to the man born blind, the Pharisees—these hypocrites—cast him out of their assembly. 'And Jesus heard that they had cast him out'—mark that, he heard it—'and when he had found him'—mark that also: he found him—'he said unto him, Dost thou believe on the Son of God? He answered and said, Who is he, Lord, that I might believe on him? And Jesus said unto him, Thou hast both seen him, and it is he that talketh with thee. And he said, Lord, I believe. And he worshipped him.' Now, that is revelation. But the poor man knew his blindness first, and that by long and bitter experience.

'Thus saith the LORD, To this man will I look, even to him that is poor and of a contrite spirit, and trembleth at my word.' 'The sacrifices of God are a broken spirit: a broken and a contrite heart, O God, thou wilt not despise.'

'For thus saith the high and lofty One that inhabiteth eternity, whose name is Holy; I dwell in the high and holy place, with him also that is of a contrite and humble spirit, to revive the spirit of the humble, and to revive the heart of the contrite ones. For I will not contend for ever, neither will I be always wroth.'

This consciousness of being born blind; this broken and contrite heart; this humble spirit; precede sonship. It is that by which sonship is ushered in. All who are of this spirit are in the secret. All these Christ shall take and build into his *ecclesia*. None other. For these he calls 'babes', and, of a truth, to them the Father reveals his Son from heaven. It is upon them that the LORD commands the blessing, even life for evermore.

This is that people, previously cut to and pricked in their heart, of whom one reads in the Acts. Upon all of these, having first received and been convicted under John's ministry, thereafter having followed Jesus, the Spirit was poured out. This is the beginning of the *ecclesia*. It was the *ecclesia* in the beginning. And it is the *ecclesia* now. As it was in the beginning, is now, and ever shall be. Amen.

JOHN METCALFE

MINISTRY BY JOHN METCALFE

TAPE MINISTRY BY JOHN METCALFE
FROM ENGLAND AND THE FAR EAST
IS AVAILABLE.

In order to obtain this free recorded ministry, please send your blank cassette (C.90) and the cost of the return postage, including your name and address in block capitals, to the John Metcalfe Publishing Trust, Church Road, Tylers Green, Penn, Bucks, HP10 8LN. Tapelists are available on request.

Owing to the increased demand for the tape ministry, we are unable to supply more than two tapes per order, except in the case of meetings for the hearing of tapes, where a special arrangement can be made.

Book Order Form

Please send to the address below:-

	Price	Quantity
A Question for Pope John Paul II	£1.25	......
Of God or Man?	£1.45	......
Noah and the Flood	£1.20	......
Divine Footsteps	£0.95	......
The Red Heifer	£0.75	......
The Wells of Salvation	£1.50	......
The Book of Ruth (Hardback edition)	£4.95	......

Psalms, Hymns & Spiritual Songs (Hardback edition)

The Psalms of the Old Testament	£2.50	......
Spiritual Songs from the Gospels	£2.50	......
The Hymns of the New Testament	£2.50	......

'Apostolic Foundation of the Christian Church' series

Foundations Uncovered	Vol.I	£0.30	......
The Birth of Jesus Christ	Vol.II	£0.95	......
The Messiah	Vol.III	£2.45	......
The Son of God and Seed of David (Hardback)	Vol.IV	£6.95	......
Christ Crucified (Hardback)	Vol.V	£6.95	......
Justification by Faith (Hardback)	Vol.VI	£7.50	......
The Church: What is it? (Hardback)	Vol.VII	£7.75	......

Name and Address (in block capitals)

. . . .

. . . .

. . . .

If money is sent with order please allow for postage. Please address to:- The John Metcalfe Publishing Trust, Church Road, Tylers Green, Penn, Bucks, HP10 8LN.

THE MINISTRY OF THE NEW TESTAMENT

The purpose of this substantial A4 gloss paper magazine is to provide spiritual and experimental ministry with sound doctrine which rightly and prophetically divides the Word of Truth.

Readers of our books will already know the high standards of our publications. They can be confident that these pages will maintain that quality, by giving access to enduring ministry from the past, much of which is derived from sources that are virtually unobtainable today, and publishing a living ministry from the present. Selected articles from the following writers have already been included:

ELI ASHDOWN · ABRAHAM BOOTH · JOHN BUNYAN
JOHN BURGON · JOHN CALVIN · DONALD CARGILL
JOHN CENNICK · J.N. DARBY · GEORGE FOX · JOHN FOXE
WILLIAM GADSBY · WILLIAM HUNTINGTON · WILLIAM KELLY
JOHN KENNEDY · HANSERD KNOLLYS · JAMES LEWIS
MARTIN LUTHER · ROBERT MURRAY MCCHEYNE · JOHN METCALFE
ALEXANDER—SANDY—PEDEN · J.C. PHILPOT · J.B. STONEY
HENRY TANNER · JOHN VINALL · JOHN WARBURTON
JOHN WELWOOD · GEORGE WHITEFIELD · J.A. WYLIE

Price £1.75 *(postage included)*
Issued Spring, Summer, Autumn, Winter.

Magazine Order Form

Name and Address (in block capitals)

. . . .

. . . .

. . . .

Please send me .... current copy/copies of The Ministry of the New Testament.

Please send me .... year/s subscription.

I enclose a cheque/postal order for £ ....

(Price: including postage, U.K. £1.75; Overseas £1.90)
(One year's subscription: Including postage, U.K. £7.00; Overseas £7.60)

Cheques should be made payable to The John Metcalfe Publishing Trust, and for overseas subscribers should be in pounds sterling drawn on a London Bank.

10 or more copies to one address will qualify for a 10% discount

Back numbers from Spring 1986 available.

Please send to The John Metcalfe Publishing Trust, Church Road, Tylers Green, Penn, Buckinghamshire, HP10 8LN.

All Publications of the Trust are subsidised by the Publishers.

Tract Order Form

Please send to the address below:-

Price Quantity

Evangelical Tracts
The Two Prayers of Elijah		£0.10	......
Wounded For Our Transgressions		£0.10	......
The Blood of Sprinkling		£0.10	......
The Grace of God That Brings Salvation		£0.10	......
The Name of Jesus		£0.10	......

'Tract for the Times' series
The Gospel of God	No.1	£0.25	......
The Strait Gate	No.2	£0.25	......
Eternal Sonship and Taylor Brethren	No.3	£0.25	......
Marks of the New Testament Church	No.4	£0.25	......
The Charismatic Delusion	No.5	£0.25	......
Premillennialism exposed	No.6	£0.25	......
Justification and Peace	No.7	£0.25	......
Faith or presumption?	No.8	£0.25	......
The Elect undeceived	No.9	£0.25	......
Justifying Righteousness	No.10	£0.25	......
Righteousness Imputed	No.11	£0.25	......
The Great Deception	No.12	£0.25	......
A Famine in the Land	No.13	£0.25	......
Blood and Water	No.14	£0.25	......
Women Bishops?	No.15	£0.25	......
The Heavenly Vision	No.16	£0.25	......

Ecclesia Tracts
The Beginning of the Ecclesia	No.1	£0.10	......
Churches and the Church (J.N.D.)	No.2	£0.10	......

Name and Address (in block capitals)

. . . .

. . . .

. . . .

If money is sent with order please allow for postage. Please address to:- The John Metcalfe Publishing Trust, Church Road, Tylers Green, Penn, Bucks, HP10 8LN.